THE ULTIMATE START-UP GUIDE

RAJ GUPTA
THE THIRD

authorHOUSE

AuthorHouse™
1663 Liberty Drive
Bloomington, IN 47403
www.authorhouse.com
Phone: 833-262-8899

© 2024 Raj Gupta The Third. All rights reserved.

No part of this book may be reproduced, stored in a retrieval system, or transmitted by any means without the written permission of the author.

Published by AuthorHouse 08/06/2024

ISBN: 979-8-8230-3128-8 (sc)
ISBN: 979-8-8230-3127-1 (e)

Library of Congress Control Number: 2024916085

Print information available on the last page.

Any people depicted in stock imagery provided by Getty Images are models, and such images are being used for illustrative purposes only. Certain stock imagery © Getty Images.

This book is printed on acid-free paper.

Because of the dynamic nature of the Internet, any web addresses or links contained in this book may have changed since publication and may no longer be valid. The views expressed in this work are solely those of the author and do not necessarily reflect the views of the publisher, and the publisher hereby disclaims any responsibility for them.

Contents

Intro: Make a Business Plan ix

Chapter 1: Mind Your Business 1

Chapter 2: What is Fear? 7

Chapter 3: Control Thy Thoughts 13

Chapter 4: Training or Certification 19

Chapter 5: Forecast Your Future with Goals 29

This book is dedicated to those who do not have faith in their start-up being a success. I have started many businesses... some were successful and some have failed. In this book, I have taken the formula on what has worked for me and how I have mastered the business plan along with the beginning stages of a start-up.

Intro

Make a Business Plan

This book will be useful to anyone that is looking to master a successful start-up. I have owned many different businesses over the past 14 years. I have mastered how to get all of these businesses started. Some of them have had massive success and others were complete failures, costing me thousands or even millions of dollars. One thing that it took… was lack of fear. Have no fear!!! Massive action and focus on the goal. Go after it, make it happen. You can accomplish it. Taking the time to read and fully utilize this book will be time well spent and putting these words into action will yield you the results you are looking for.

I have written at least a hundred business plans and not all of those businesses even came into action. Even at the age of 16, I was so motivated to be successful. I saw something or had an idea and I wanted to write a business plan. Getting your ideas on paper to look at and read helps with the creative process. A business plan can be one page or one hundred pages. It really depends on the scope of your business. I will say that if you plan on asking someone for $100,000 or more, you should have more than 20 pages.

You should invest more time in thinking and planning before you begin to take action. I know a lot of people say, "Well, I have been in this industry for years and I know everything about this industry. All I need is the money." The business plan is important because it communicates, to everyone involved in the organization, what the goals are and how management will get there.

At Leavey School of Business, the My Own Business Institute (MOBI) program provides online education tools for entrepreneurs around the world. Its website generates roughly 70,000 page views each month. Business owners can register for a web course and earn a certificate for free. MOBI also offers a downloadable business plan template, which is designed to help start-ups in any sector, from bakeries to IT services.

The parts that make up a business plan are straightforward. According to guidelines from the U.S. Small Business Administration, you need to include the following:

- An executive summary
- A company description
- A market analysis
- An organization and management breakdown
- A description of the service or product line
- An overview of your marketing strategy
- A request for funding
- Some financial projections to back up your ask
- Relevant resumes, permits, or leases.

Chapter 1

Mind Your Business

The first step is to simply describe the business you want to build. During the process, it's important to be honest about the obstacles you're likely to face.

Start throwing out ideas and suggestions, including a breakdown of the target market and customers. You should also be clear about the factors offering a competitive edge.

Be careful not to have any blinders on when it comes to your product or service. "People spend a lot of time focusing on the features that make them unique without taking the time to translate that into a value proposition," says Starbird.

Do diligent research on what your market is and how to communicate with customers accordingly. "The most successful investors are looking for an idea that is going to have a clear and understandable market potential," he adds.

Secondly, have a thorough plan: Document all aspects of your company. Starbird also states, "As the founder, you need to be concerned about all parts of the plan." That means including any licensing agreements or your location strategy, for example.

It's especially important to know and understand your numbers. "The number one reason firms go under is inadequate cash flow. If you don't know what's going on in that area, you're going to be in big trouble," Starbird warns.

Third, make sure the plan is modifiable for different audiences. Different sections of your business plan will be more important depending on your audience. Investors, for instance, will want to see your financial projections, whereas employees might be more concerned with the organizational structure of your company.

The SBA recommends that you project that status of your company for between three and five years into the future, though it's a good idea to outline your annual goals, too. Keep in mind that the further ahead you look, the less accurate your conclusions are going to be.

"A five-year horizon is fine, but a thorough business plan looks beyond that (up to 10 years), with the recognition that some of the forecasts would be of decreasing accuracy," says Starbird. He recommends updating your business plan every year as the company grows.

Fourth, include details to put you over the edge.

When writing the market analysis, it's a good idea to include any information about external growth trends and why one company might have the market share. Pricing power- how consumer demand would be affected if your company shifted its prices- is one detail that often gets excluded from business plans, but which can help put you over the edge.

It's also important to keep your expectations realistic and honest. "The biggest mistake entrepreneurs can make when writing a business plan," says Starbird, "is to be overly optimistic with sales and future cost estimates."

Fifth, remember why you care.

At Hall & Rambo, Starbird stated that his primary role was to be the "gopher guy." It allowed him to learn the ropes of running a business and to prioritize goals beyond the bottom line. "It was very clear working with my father and grandfather and uncle that it wasn't just about making money," he said. Other priorities included raising the payroll for employees, offering competitive benefits and making an impact on the local Central California community.

Your business plan should reflect not only your financial goals but also your values and those of the community you're working to build.

Get Rid of Fear and Take Action

As I have been told many times, the only thing to fear is fear itself. Why be scared? So many drop the momentum and motivation before they even get started. This is a quick reminder to not give up before anything has happened. The drive and ambition that you have to start a business, allow yourself time to bring it into action.

How many times have you wanted to take action but ended up procrastinating? I know we are all guilty of this. Yet, it's what makes the difference between the people who "want something to happen" from those who "make it happen."

It's not that successful people don't procrastinate. It's just that they get back up on their feet, despite these personal setbacks. If you want to get more confidence, achieve more success and realize your dreams, then learning to get back on your feet and take action is the way.

Today you'll learn why people fear taking action, why taking action is the antidote to fear and 7 tips to get you back on your feet even after you have procrastinated.

Let's dive in!

Why Most People Fear to Take Action

We know that procrastination leads to more frustration in the future, yet everyone is guilty of it at times and that's not a big issue, it's part of life. However, when procrastination becomes a habit, that's a bit of an issue. Research shows that it reduces self-confidence and performance. That's a big downside if you want to create a better life for yourself.

So why do people procrastinate anyway? People fear action because they're worried that the result is more painful than the pain they experience from procrastination. That is due to two things: fear and desire.

Chapter 2

What is Fear?

Fear is the most common reason to avoid action. The most common fears include: the fear of rejection, the fear of failure, and even the fear of success.

Change makes people fearful because the unknown is scary and unconsciously avoiding pain gets the priority over pleasure, from a "survival" point of view. You know how the situation looks worse within your mind than it turns out to be in reality? We give too much credit to the worst possible outcomes.

For myself, presenting is scary as hell. Every time I present, my legs are shaking, my hands begin sweating and I start to talk faster. Meanwhile, every time I finish, I just think:

Was that it?

It's not as scary as I imagine it to be. Even though my fears become reality sometimes, it's never as big of a deal as I imagined. I mean, sometimes I stumble over my own words or I can't find the right thing to say but I always make it out of the presentation alive.

What I'm trying to say is that even the outcomes that you are fearful of, they often aren't as bad as you've made up in your mind. Still, these fears often take over our internal dialogue. That's why we rather delay than start taking action.

"I'll need a little more experience before I can do this."

"The time isn't right today."

"I'm not sure if this is the path to follow."

Doubt, doubt and more doubt.

Desire

A lack of desire is the counterpart of fear. This is because if you lack a desire for the result, you're far less likely to face your challenges and overcome fear. Think about that for a second.

Let's say that you're cold calling people in a sales job from 9 to 5 and you need to hit three sales that day to get your bonus. By 2 pm, you've just hit your third sale and secured your bonus. The question for you to answer honestly is: Would you stop and take off the rest of the day or would you continue, immediately up your goal to 5 and keep pushing like you have never pushed before?

If you would keep pushing, you have the required desire to make it in a startup! Those small decisions are what will make the difference between surviving and thriving. Having a burning desire is fundamental to taking massive action.

Thinking Will Not Overcome Fear, Taking Action Will

When you tell yourself that you're *not ready yet* or waiting for *a better moment,* you miss out on great opportunities because the truth is, you'll never feel 100% ready.

The paradox is, that you only become more prepared for other opportunities if you persist through the discomfort of the opportunity that's ahead of you.

Fear Never Goes Away

It's scary to think that you'll always experience a certain degree of fear but it's only scary because you hope that the fear goes away- and you know that won't happen. The antidote to fear is not to dismiss it, but to change your relationship with it.

Don't expect fear to go away but learn that you can live beside fear. Everyone misses opportunities because they think that the next opportunity becomes easier if they read one more book or watch one more YouTube video but the goal isn't to get rid of fear. The goal is to embrace fear and take action even though you experience it.

I once listened to a professional public speaker talk about fear, who had been on stage for Decennia. Here's what he said (approximately): "Every time I'm about to jump on stage, I experience levels of anxiety and fear but I've done this so many times that I've learned that I can deal with what comes next."

Start Taking Action

Taking action despite fear is your fast track to more self-confidence, success and even happiness.

Once the action becomes a habit, the action becomes automatic. That's when you no longer overthink the possible outcomes but you just do it. That's also when fear no longer holds you back but instead becomes your trigger for action.

Let's dive into quick reasons to understand the truth.

Understand the Truth

The interview with the professional public speaker who said that he still experiences fear before going on stage was a real eye-opener for me. If you're surprised by his answer too, then this tip is very useful for you because with the wrong expectation about fear, you're expecting an outcome that will never come.

So, here's the truth one more time: Fear never goes away. Instead, you get better at taking action despite fear. That's what gives you the level of confidence that you need to deal with whatever happens next.

When you deeply understand this truth, you create a better relationship with fear.

Appreciate the Sensation of Fear

We stay with the relationship between you and fear for a second- but take it a step deeper. Not only should you become okay with the experience of fear, you should embrace it. So, any time that you experience the sensation of fear (in non-life-threatening situations of course), understand that this is a great indicator of personal success.

Your growth demands you to get outside of your comfort zone and push your boundaries. Taking action through fear is the "quick-fix" to self-improvement.

Chapter 3

Control Thy Thoughts

I love philosophy when it's also super practical in everyday life. One of the most practical pieces I've read comes from the philosophy of the Stoics.

The practical lesson is this: Focus on what you can control and learn to accept that which isn't in your control.

Too often people become obsessed with things that happen in their life over which they have no control. For example, when you can't continue working because Carol first has to deliver her piece of research for a project. Here's another common one: When the traffic light turns red just as you get close. Becoming upset with these situations, only has downsides.

First, you're not likely to change the situation by becoming mad (if anything, you'll make it worse) and second, you're clouding your mind with negativity. Shifting your focus on things you can't control makes you feel powerless.

Things happen in life. Accept what you can't control and take action on what you can control. Learning to think this way, is the road to mental freedom.

With a fixed mindset, you believe that everything is as it is. You are either good at something or you're not. With this mindset, you believe that talent plays a key role in one's success. A growth mindset is quite the opposite. You see the world as a playground for learning and you believe that you can learn anything if you're willing to spend the time and energy.

The biggest difference in taking action is the connection to fear. With a fixed mindset, you're fearful of mistakes. You may feel as if you fail, it means you're incapable and that's quite a hit to the ego. Thus, not trying is much safer than trying and failing.

The growth mindset embraces mistakes. After all, the world is your playground. You know that when you step outside of your comfort zone, you're going to make mistakes no matter how good you are. A growth mindset allows you to take action, whereas a fixed mindset freezes you.

Take Action Early

Willpower is a valuable resource and helps you to take action in the short-term so that you can enjoy greater benefits in the long-term. The problem with willpower is that it's a resource that you use throughout the day. Leaving you with less willpower in the tank at night, versus the morning.

This makes you more vulnerable to snacking in the evening, for example. It also makes you less likely to take action later in the day, especially when you haven't formed a habit yet. Let's say that you want to become a better writer, practicing it every day and deciding to write a little article every evening. How high do you estimate your chances to stay consistent with this?

If you're like most people, you'll often end up enjoying your time watching Netflix or spending your time with friends instead of writing. What would happen if you write first thing in the morning though? Your willpower is at its highest point, meaning you're less likely to swap it for an episode of your favorite Netflix series and your friends are still asleep.

On top of that, when you do this in the morning, you've already got a reason to feel great that day. By the time everyone else wakes up, you've already taken action on your desires. Soon writing becomes a new habit in your life that doesn't need much willpower at all.

Waking up a bit earlier and making time to do this isn't easy, but it's much easier than trying to take action later in the day.

Remove Distractions

There's nothing worse than motivating yourself to get started and getting distracted straight after you take action. What happens mentally when you start writing early in the morning but decide to check social media for 5 minutes?

It's never just 5 minutes… right?

Getting rid of potential distractions is a great way to get work done. After you have worked hard and got things done, then use your distractions as rewards for taking action.

First, start by learning what those distractions are for you. Is it a notification on your phone or laptop? Try airplane mode or put these devices away if you don't need them at all. Do you keep getting distracted by a messy room or desk? You know what to do.

If you get distracted, don't worry or beat yourself up over it. Take care of the distraction so that it won't happen again in the future.

Chapter 4

Training or Certification

This chapter is for the individual or individuals who believe they want to take on a new industry that they have no expertise or experience in. This does create a larger risk but a massive reward so, go for it. No fear will ever come from my words to you. A lot of people are told to play it safe but, why? We are here to live this life, not in lack but in abundance. Be proud of what we have done here on this Earth.

We are taught to play it safe so we can make smart decisions but smart decisions will yield you results that are what? What do they equate to? A boring fucking life! NO. DON'T EVEN WASTE TIME THINKING ABOUT PLAYING IT SAFE.

If you're reading this book and you want to become a business owner, be the best business owner you can be and live in abundance. Out work everyone in the space and create a better product than is on the current market. We all have our moment; the problem is we think we need to be experts in the field before we start to create something.

You need to do self-education. If there are courses or certifications needed, then do it. The number one thing you will need is belief in yourself and that's 90% of the training or certification you will ever need.

Certification is Motivating

Get a certification if you feel you NEED it. It can be motivating, accomplishing and taking on a new challenge of learning. I encourage you to do so if you are new in the space that you're in and you need an extra boost of confidence.

Be careful! Getting certification gives a false sense of reality. You may have felt prepared by the knowledge you have acquired from your certification in the new field, but it has also taken time away from getting more experience to become comfortable with running your business day to day. Experience is often times more valuable.

Secure Funding (The Bag)

Explore how small business loans, microloans and loan programs help you get started. Decide on a business structure and consider which is best for you- sole proprietorship, partnership, corporation or nonprofit. Then, choose a name. It's essential for marketing. Use your own name or you'll need to register a "Doing Business As" (DBA) name. Pay your taxes. You should be aware that in addition to paying federal business taxes, your business will also have to pay income and employment taxes, plus certain state and local taxes.

Preparation is crucial to finding the funding you need. This step is often overlooked, but unless you want to be constantly pumping your own resources into your business, you'll want to assess and address various aspects of your company to ensure its overall readiness.

Not only will you need to examine your team's overall health from every angle, but to research your industry, competitors and the market, define your products, prepare financial projections and determine how much money to raise, plus decide whether to tap into debt or equity.

Preparation may be the most time-consuming and effort-intensive aspect of raising funds but if you know what you want and outline the rationale behind those choices, you'll find it easier to figure out whom to target and ask for what you need.

Remember, as you court investors, they will be asking the tough questions. So, you'll have to be equipped with all the relevant information you need.

Related: My first successful venture was a start-up where my partner suppled $15,000.00 in credit line and 2 years later, she had a 600% ROI based on that investment and 30 hours of work for her for the year, pretty fair trade off. If you have a great business idea, plan, network and put the business plan in front of angel investors, banks or anyone that has a credit line or access to capital, you can make it happen if you don't give up. Don't ever get discouraged based on anyone rejecting your idea or business. It is up to you to believe in yourself more than anyone.

Researching the Different Types of Investors

Just because you've decided whom you're going to go after and what amount to ask, it doesn't necessarily mean you're going to get what you've requested. When it comes to financial matters, the more options you can identify, the better. That way, you'll always have a backup plan when you need it.

Among the different types of investors that you may consider, there are: Founders, family, friends, venture capitalists, angel investors, single family offices, business incubators, investment groups and crowdfunding pledgers.

Keeping in mind that some forms of funding are costlier and riskier than others, you can also use credit cards, lines of credit, bank loans and the like. These financing options are often last resorts or backup initiatives, as they are more contingent on the condition of your personal finances and assets, versus the value or potential value of your business.

Getting Your Pitch Deck Ready

Much has already been said about the necessity of a pitch deck and the ways in which to put together an effective presentation. The fundamentals are that your presentation should be used to highlight the most attractive aspects of your business. Keeping your target audience in mind and knowing what's important to investors is key.

Generally, 10 to 15 slides containing information on your company, your team, competition, target market, milestones, future plans and funding requirements will be sufficient. Armed with this information, your prospective investors should be better able to decide on a course of action that's in alignment with their best interests.

Networking and Finding Potential Investors

You can never know too many people. While networking, you don't necessarily need to be constantly promoting your business, you should just make sure you are helping other people. This will help you garner a positive reputation and when you help others get what they want, they will be more likely to help you.

Keep in mind that you will face rejection when discussing your business with others. Some investors may not be looking for an opportunity right now. For other people, your concept simply won't be the right fit. Knowing this going in can save you a lot of heartache and stress.

Obtain Necessary Licenses and Permits

There are federal and state licenses and permits you will need to obtain to legally run your business. Researching various investment groups and resources online can prove worthwhile. Just don't get sucked into the bottomless blackhole of the internet. Try making a phone call or sending emails, so that you remain proactive when reaching out.

Finding Companies That Offer Capital in Your Niche

If you have a niche business model aligned with ecommerce or SaaS, or say you produce devices for the healthcare industry, you can find investors that offer funding to those types of companies.

This isn't to suggest you won't need to look for additional sources of funding, but if finding tailored solutions streamlines your process of finding capital, it will be worth looking into.

Final Thoughts

Even with all of your ducks in a row, there are no guarantees you'll get the capital you need from the investors you're courting but problem-solving is part and parcel of entrepreneurship. Knowing all of your options and what you can do to get the money you need can give you greater confidence when you encounter bumps in the road. Bumps, unfortunately, are something you can count on experiencing.

Be compliant with key federal and state regulations. It will be essential when you hire employees. Contact the U.S. Small Business Administration (SBA). Your local SBA website can give you more detailed information as well.

Work Through the Beginning Phase

Work through the pain and don't focus on "What if I fail?" Focus on "What will I do with the money when I succeed?" Have a plan. Allow the success of your start-up to become something you focus on.

In the beginning, you may have to take on six different positions. Embrace this moment. This will build character; this will build confidence in that you don't need anyone to help you through your pit fails. If someone leaves you as an employee, don't worry about it, you know how to cover the position if you need to. You also have the power to train everyone in each position if you need to.

Find the Areas of Weakness

Find out your area of weakness in the 30 days after you have launched your startup and analyze the area you need the most help with. It's important to know your areas of strength but very important to know your areas of weakness.

Chapter 5

Forecast Your Future with Goals

Setting goals is the last chapter in this book because it is the last thing you should be thinking about. Without the chapters above, you have nothing to set if there is no business. Success leaves clues and any ship going to a destination has to have direction. Where do you want to go? How soon do you want to get there? What action plan are you willing to do to get there?

How To Set Short-term Business Goals

Short-term business goals are typically goals that you want your company to achieve in a period of weeks or months. The following are steps you can take when setting short-term business goals:

1. Identify your company's short-term business goals for a set period of time

The first step in setting short-term business goals is to figure out which goals you want to achieve in a set period of time. Many short-term goals are goals that further the achievement of long-term goals. Consider your long-term goals as well with what you want to accomplish in the next weeks or months and translate these into short-term goals that will propel your business forward.

2. Break down each goal into actionable business objectives

Next, you should break down each short-term goal into actionable objectives. These objectives should represent the steps your company will take to reach each goal. For example, if your goal is to get six new customers in the next month, your objectives will be the steps you will take to secure the business of six customers. This may include putting a new ad in a newspaper and posting three times a week on social media.

3. Ensure your objectives are measurable

The business objectives you establish in the previous step need to be measurable. For example, if one of your objectives to reach a short-term goal is to post more on social media, don't simply state *"post more on social media"* as a strategy. Instead, make the objective measurable by being as specific as possible. Using the above example, you could use *"post on Instagram three times a week and Facebook two times a week for eight weeks."*

4. Assign goal-related tasks to employees

Once you have established the objectives for each short-term goal, assign each objective to an employee or team of employees who will see the objective through to completion.

5. Measure progress regularly

Regularly measure the progress of your short-term goals to ensure you are on track to meeting them in the time frame you established. For example, if you increase your social media posts to three times a week as part of a business goal, measure any increased customer/potential customer interaction you receive as a result. Keep track of the progress and adjust your objectives, if needed, to better meet your goals.

Examples Of Short-term Business Goals

Here are a few examples of short-term business goals:

- Increase product prices by 3% over the next three months.
- Hire three new marketing employees over the next five months.
- Increase traffic on your company's blog.
- Implement monthly giveaways for customers on social media.
- Begin an "Employee of the Month" award program.
- Select a charity to begin sponsoring.
- Create a profile on a new social media channel.
- Increase social media posting to three times a week.

How To Set Long-term Business Goals

In addition to the steps mentioned in the section on how to set short-term goals, you should also include these steps when creating long-term business goals:

1. Establish the goals you want to accomplish over the next 10 years

The first step to creating long-term business goals is to determine the goals you want to accomplish over the next several years. Many people find that setting goals 10 years out is sufficient, however, you can set goals as little as one year out or as far away as 20 years. Identify and write down as many goals as possible that you want your business to achieve in the time period you decide on.

2. Prioritize your long-term business goals

Many companies have several goals that they want to accomplish in the long-term. However, it's difficult to focus on every goal at once. For this reason, it's important to prioritize the goals that you want to focus on first and put your company resources into accomplishing those before moving onto other goals.

3. Break down each long-term goal into short-term objectives

Similar to how you break down short-term goals, you will also need to break down your long-term goals into actionable short-term objectives. For example, if your long-term goal is to increase your company's overall brand awareness, you will need to break this down into short-term objectives that will ultimately help you accomplish the long-term goal. Examples of actionable objectives for the above goal would be to post to social media three times a week and collaborate with social media influencers on a monthly basis.

4. Track your company's long-term goals regularly

An important component of accomplishing long-term goals is tracking them on a regular basis. Because long-term goals can take an extended period of time to reach, it can be easy to forget about them or lose sight of the end goal. Keeping track of the progress being made towards each goal can ensure that you're on the right path to reaching these goals and enable you to make any adjustments when needed.

Examples Of Long-term Business Goals

The following are examples of long-term business goals:

- Increase the total income of your company by 10% over the next two years.
- Reduce production expenses by 5% over the next three years.
- Increase overall brand awareness.
- Increase your company's share in its market.
- Open three new office locations throughout the United States.
- Hire 50 new employees nationwide.
- Develop and launch three new products.

Believe In Your Plan

It is very likely that you will face some challenging times while you are in the process of building your business. With any challenge or obstacle, you're able to find an answer. That's why the challenge is there for you to overcome. Let me give you an example:

In my first business in door-to-door sales, I had an issue with hiring, with ads and no one, I mean NO ONE was showing up to interviews. If I didn't hire at least 2-3 reps a week, my business would die. 3-4 WEEKS in, potential employees were still failing to show. This caused me to negotiate a partnership with a local company that worked in the same field. I offered to compensate them for every person they hired in the area that benefited me and in order to balance the costly expense of that, I sent my recruiting team to watch and learn from their team.

We monitored what they were doing for three weeks, replicated it at my office and bam! Recruiting went up 100% and we began increasing revenue. Don't be afraid to build relationships with your competition in other markets if you own a business. The power of networking is one that will be stronger than any quick buck you can make. I have done a lot of things on my own but I have had both great mentors in my life and poor mentors. I have learned something valuable from each one of them.

Believe in the plan and yourself. This is the greatest way to start a business. Take the time, write it out and think about it daily. Read and write it over and over and watch the magic happen.

www.ingramcontent.com/pod-product-compliance
Lightning Source LLC
Chambersburg PA
CBHW031553210526
45464CB00003B/1283